Ely
Life As A Service Dog Puppy

Written by Margot Bennett

with help from Ely

Copyright © 2022 by Margot Bennett.

All rights reserved worldwide. No part of this publication may be reproduced, distributed or transmitted in any form or by any means, including photocopying, recording, or other electronic or mechanical methods, without the prior written permission of the publisher, except in the case of brief quotations embodied in critical reviews and certain other noncommercial uses permitted by copyright law. Please do not participate in or encourage piracy of copyrighted materials in violation of the author's rights. Purchase only authorized editions.

For permission requests, email tailsofdogswhohelp@gmail.com

Story and photography by Margot Bennett
Cover photo by Brian Batista Photography
Chapter 10 photography by Canine Companions®
Duke Puppy Kindergarten photo by Jared Lazarus
Photo modifications created using Photo Lab
Book design by Sarah E. Holroyd (https://sleepingcatbooks.com)

Ely, Life As A Service Dog Puppy/Margot Bennett — 1st ed.
Published May 2022
LCCN: 2022904433
Hardcover ISBN: 978-1-7357990-3-2
Paperback ISBN: 978-1-7357990-4-9
Ebook ISBN: 978-1-7357990-5-6

Produced in the United States of America

This book is dedicated to all those involved in the journey to becoming a service dog- breeder caretakers, puppy raisers, trainers, donors, administrative staff and of course, the graduates. Graduates are provided service dogs at no cost thanks to all those involved in the puppy raising experience. Canine Companion puppies are loved and cared for from before they are even born, until they have passed over the rainbow bridge.

I hope you enjoy the journey of one of these amazing dogs, Ely.

Proceeds from Ely, Life As A Service Dog Puppy are donated to Canine Companions to assist in providing training for present and future service dogs.

Other books by Margot Bennett

Tails Of Dogs Who Help Series
Brisco, Life As A Therapy Dog, Book 1

Hello! My name is Ely and I am a yellow Labrador Retriever.

I am a service dog to an amazing woman named Miranda. Her bones and joints cause her a lot of pain and my job is to help her with tasks like:

- Picking things up from the floor
- Tugging open doors
- Pulling off socks
- Turning light switches on/off

I even help with laundry! I pull things out of the washer and put them in the dryer for her. When we are done with our chores, Miranda and I love to snuggle. Snuggles are way more important than stinky socks.

I trained for a long time to become the handsome and professional dog I am today.

I am excited to share my story!

Chapter 1
Ely's First Puppy Home

I was born in California with six brothers and sisters, all with names that began with the letter "E."

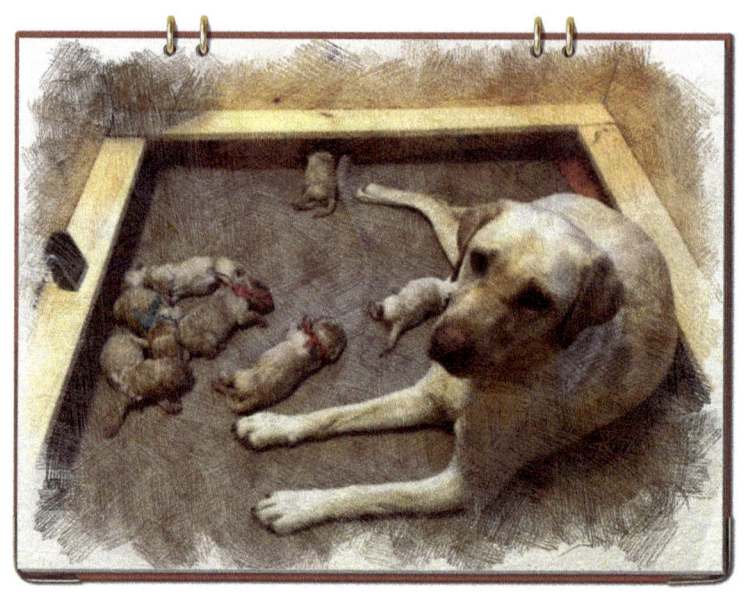

Elvie

Emma

Einstein

Eugene

Electra

Endo

And of course me, Ely!

Can you think of any other names that begin with E?

When we were first born, our caretakers carefully wrapped a ribbon on each of us. The different colors displayed what order we were born in. I was born third so I showed off the color purple!

Which one is me?

When puppies are born, we cannot see or hear very well. Sometimes our legs are wobbly and we stumble around a lot.

When we got tired, we tumbled into small, puppy piles and fell asleep. Our dreams were filled with hopes to someday run as fast as the wind. My siblings snored loudly beside me. Sometimes this kept me awake for hours!

Dog-mom, Ruscha, always kept us safe and warm inside our dog playpen.

What do you remember seeing and hearing when you were little?

Section: Learning To Play

As weeks passed, my brothers and sisters and I grew stronger and began to play with each other.

Just like human babies, we learned through play. Our caretakers provided us with all sorts of things to play with in our puppy playpen.

Hanging toys to swat at!

Bumpy ramps to climb up and down!

Toy slides to scramble down!

All these activities played an important role in helping to build our confidence. We learned about our bodies and to get back up when we fell down.

Section: Learning Sounds

As the days passed, we began to hear new noises throughout the day and night. Our caretakers made sure to introduce us to all sorts of things.

- Washing machines whirred
- Babies cried
- Sirens rang
- Thunderstorms clapped

We were too busy with puppy piles and playtime to be bothered by the sounds in the background.

What noises do you hear often at your house?

Sometimes we took a break during our days to pose for family pictures.

Oops!

Blooper!

Oh dear!

We just could not sit still for the camera. Our dog-mom, Ruscha, was disappointed we were not able to pose politely, but she loved us dearly. She understood we were just a busy bunch of E's.

Section: Meal Time and More

My favorite part of the day was meal time. My brothers and sisters and I danced around the food bowl in a frenzy as our tails wagged excitedly. *Slurp, Slurp, Gulp.* We licked our bowls clean.

Is there any more? We looked up at our caretakers and wagged our tails hopefully, but sadly, no more food until next time.

Every day, visitors of all ages came to stroke our ears, massage our paws, and rub our bellies.

Puppy naps? Those were included too!

From the very beginning, there was always a lap to curl up in.

Our lives were filled with so many people who helped take care of us.

"Good boy," someone praised me as I lay quietly while they brushed my fur.

"You are going to be such a good service dog," said someone else as I brought back a tennis ball I had chased across the room.

Our puppy days were filled with playtime, meals, noises and naps. All these things played a part in helping us even when we were little to be successful as a future service dog.

I did not know what a service dog was then. I just knew I was having fun learning new things!

Do you think Ely has learned everything he needs to yet?

Chapter 2
The First Step in My Journey

Before I knew it, I was eight weeks old and ready for the next step in my service dog training. I overheard my caretaker reading a letter out loud. It was an announcement being sent to my puppy raiser, a woman named Margot.

Meet Ely—Arriving January 6, 2019!

The next part of my journey!

I wonder if she is excited to meet me?

I learned later that not only was my puppy raiser super excited but that she had spent months preparing for me to arrive, getting things like special food and toys, even nail clippers, a bed, a toothbrush, and more.

I needed a lot of stuff!

She also read many articles and books about the training and care I would need to prepare me to be a service dog.

Will I be able to remember everything she teaches me?

Section: Leaving Home

On our last morning, my caretakers gave me a bath and brushed my fur until it was silky smooth. My brothers and sisters were all cleaned up too. We were all flying to different parts of the country to be with our puppy raisers.

I ran around with my brothers and sisters all morning! We chased each other around the yard to stretch our legs before the long airplane ride. Then suddenly, it was time to leave. My caretakers gave me lots of hugs and kisses as they placed me into my puppy carrier. I could feel lots of love surrounding me as I got ready to leave.

A few puppy tears trickled down my face at leaving my first home, but I felt ready for this big adventure. I was excited, but also nervous.

Can you think of a time when you were nervous to go somewhere new?

Questions swirled around my puppy head.

Who will I play with?

Where will I sleep?

Will there be toys?

The constant buzzing and vibrations of the engine soon lulled my worries to sleep. When I woke up, I peeked and saw the sun.

I was here!

My tummy rumbled. *When is dinner?*

Section: Meeting My New Family

I sniffed the air around me. My new home had a warm, familiar smell to it.

I wonder if there are other dogs here?

Suddenly, the door to my crate opened and warm, soft hands gently lifted me up and cradled me.

I peeked and saw a woman with short, brown hair. I heard her soft voice talk to me. "Hi, sweet Ely," she cooed, as she rubbed the fur on my neck, back and forth.

"Welcome to your new home! I'm Margot, your puppy raiser."

Puppy raiser? I'm here!

I felt so warm and safe. My whole body relaxed and I felt my eyelids getting heavy.

Suddenly, I was scooped up with squeals of delight from children. As they cuddled me, I watched two large dogs, one yellow and one white, trot over and sit by the door.

I knew I smelled dogs, I need to meet them!

I wriggled to be let down.

"What is your name?" I asked the older one as I plopped myself next to him.

"Brisco," he whispered. "Woof! Welcome!"

The lady-dog had fur as white as snow. She spoke her name to me quietly, "I'm Aspen."

I sat nervously, not sure what to say to my new fur family. I tried to count in my head how many paws were in my new home.

How many paws can YOU count in the picture?

Hmmm. What should I do now?

Section: Exploring My New Home

My two new friends got up and moved so I decided to follow them.
I swatted at Brisco's tail.
Who needs toys when you have a tail to play with!

Soon I tired of this activity and needed to run off my puppy energy.

What should I do next?

I decided to explore my new home by zooming up and down the hallways. The children giggled and followed me. I ran from room to room like a hockey puck sliding across the ice. Swooosh! Swooosh!

In my excitement, I scrambled up the steps. I sat there, still like a statue, unsure of what to do.

I glanced up to the top of the stairs and heard Brisco's calm voice.

"Woof," he called down to me, gently. "Be brave, you can make it back down."

Nervously, I stretched out one paw and then another. Suddenly, my paw slipped over the edge and I pulled it back. I tried again.

Hooray! I felt the floor under my feet. Soon, I was walking up and down all thirteen steps without being scared at all!

All this curiosity was exhausting and I was thirsty. I bolted to the water bowl for a drink, but Brisco was already there.

"Woof, ahem," his voice rumbled. "Me first, Ely."
So I waited for him to finish.

Section: Outside

Next, my family introduced me to my new backyard where I saw lots of trees, a swingset and a huge wooden fort. It was just like my puppy playpen, but bigger!

With enthusiasm, I sprinted up the long, wooden ramp.

I felt so big and tall in the fort. I felt so high in the sky and so brave!

Not only could I see way over Aspen's head, I could see rooftops two streets over! "Woof," Brisco whispered to me from below. "Time to come down."

I began to realize that not only was Brisco my new friend, he was also trying to help me learn. I had a puppy raiser AND a big brother!

At the end of the first few days in my new home, I collapsed from exhaustion.

I leaned into my new puppy raiser as she held me. After a few minutes of snuggling, she carried me to a puppy kennel and tucked me in for the night. I wrapped myself into a ball, feeling loved.

I missed my brothers, sisters, and dog-mom, but I dreamed of smelling new things, seeing new sights, and loving my new family.

What will be the first thing I learn?

Chapter 3
Ely Learns His First Commands

Training to be a service dog began on my very first morning.

"Sit," my puppy raiser said as she poured food into a bowl. Drool dribbled down my chin as I waited, and waited, and waited for my meal.

What were some of the first words you learned growing up?

"Woof," Brisco whispered to me. "Be patient."
"I am trying!" I woofed back.
My tummy rumbled. Waiting was so hard!

"Down," my puppy raiser said later as we stopped in the hallway.

"Woof," Brisco whispered to me. "Lay on the floor." Look who joined me!

Can you tell which one is me?

"Let's go!" My puppy raiser said as she stood next to me, facing forward.

"Woof," Brisco whispered behind me. "Follow her."

I began walking with her. My voice carried back to Brisco. "Look at me!" I pranced my paws up and down on the driveway as I stopped and started when she did.

Section: MORE New Words

As I grew older and my body became stronger, I began to learn commands that would be used to help my partner with tasks.

"Drop," my puppy raiser said, as I picked up a leaf with my mouth.

"Woof," Brisco whispered. "Push that out of your mouth."

Oh dear. Am I not allowed to put things from the yard in my mouth?

I did not want to be naughty.

My puppy raiser laughed when I had to stick my tongue out several times to push the crunchy leaf out of my mouth.

Sometimes I learned a command that my partner would need to take care of me!

"Roll." my puppy raiser said, after she told me to lay down.

"Woof," Brisco whispered to me. "Turn on your back."

This made me feel silly. Was my puppy raiser going to tickle me on my belly?

Slowly, her fingers glided over my belly and I relaxed. My legs flopped to the floor. After she clipped my toenails, my puppy raiser also rubbed something yummy against my teeth.

Chicken flavored toothpaste!
Have YOU ever tried chicken flavored toothpaste?
What will be next?

Chapter 4
Ely Learns to Wear His Vest

I had gotten used to feeling the harness and leash being placed on me as we practiced our short walks in the driveway. One morning, my puppy raiser gave the command, "Dress." She encouraged me to put my head through an opening in a yellow vest.

I felt a gentle tug as the strap was fastened under my belly. "It is time for you to start going out into the world, Ely," my puppy raiser said. There was a hint of adventure in her voice.

I wagged my tail with excitement.

Thump Thump.

I felt so official in my new training vest!

Do you have certain clothes you only wear on special occasions? How do they make you feel?

The vest had special words and pictures on it that showed people I was learning to work.

I would learn there were special rules when I wore my vest. I could not say hi to people or sniff things. I always had to pay attention to my puppy raiser.

My heart fluttered with anticipation as I moved to this next level of training.

I looked in the mirror and thought to myself, *"Wow! I am so handsome!"*

I imagined myself in the future as a service dog for someone.

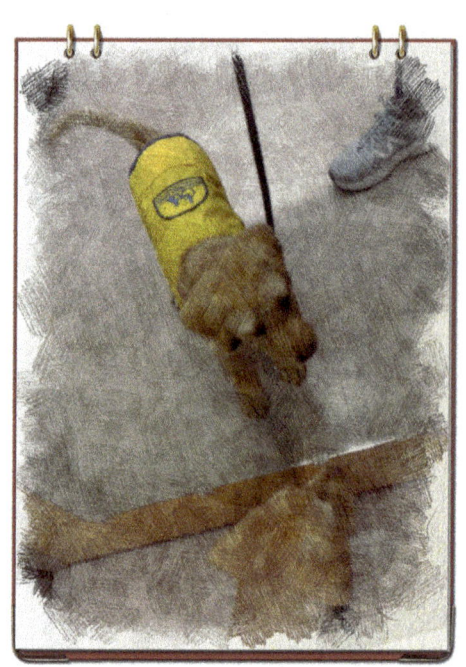

A hero!
I stood up a little straighter.

I wonder what things I might do for my partner when I am a service dog?

Section: Service Dog Class

I began going to puppy class with other dogs just like me. We all wore our official vests and practiced around all sorts of distractions–including each other! Without playing!

That was hard–I just wanted to wrestle a little!

"Under," spoke my puppy raiser, and I crawled beneath a rack. Hanging clothes kept me hidden. *I am a hibernating bear!*

"Heel," she said. I moved to her left side. I sat still as a statue. *I am playing freeze tag!*

"Up," cheered my puppy raiser. I lifted my front paws up onto the ledge of a fish tank. I watched as the fish made bubbles when they swam by. *I am a ship captain!*

Why do you think Ely needs to learn the command Up?

At the end of class, my friends and I had worked hard together. We were allowed to say hi to each other, and then posed for a picture.

Can you smile and say 'dog biscuit' like we did?

I proudly walked by my puppy raiser's side back to the car. Puppy class is almost as fun as snuggling in my puppy raiser's lap......almost.

Where might I go next?

Chapter 5
Ely's Training Adventures

I now wore my training vest everywhere I went with my puppy raiser. She took me to so many places! I walked by her side and saw all sorts of things.

She would bring me places so I could experience:
- Traffic—The noisy engines and honking!
- Parks—The running children and huge slides!
- Elevators—Oh that jumpy tummy feeling!

Sometimes I would get nervous and lag behind her. She always spoke to me in a calm and loving voice, "Ely, Let's go!" Her cheerful, smiling face was enough for me to know I could do anything. I learned to be calm and have all my attention on my puppy raiser.

She was absolutely my #1!

Service dogs must always focus on their partner. For this reason, if you ever come into contact with a service dog or service dog in training, you must not interact with them in any way. Interacting with a dog that is working or training could put the other half of the team—the handler—in harm's way.

Section: First Office Visit

Office visits are an important thing for service dogs to learn how to settle at, so one morning we drove to my puppy raisers' dentist. I followed her from the car into the exam room.

"Down," I heard, and I lay right by my puppy raiser. She sat in a huge chair under a bright light. My tummy had butterflies.

What was I expected to do?

I heard tool-grinding noises, water running, and music playing. I had heard all sorts of sounds when I was little so they did not bother me.

In fact, as I listened to all the noises floating around the room, I began to get bored and soon fell asleep.

I dreamed about flying through oodles of kibble and snorted myself awake. My puppy raiser looked down at me. "Ely, release. We're all done!"

That was easy.

Check! One more step closer to being a service dog!

At the end of every day, I found Brisco for a short snuggle and quickly fell asleep.

"Thank you so much for helping me, Brisco," I whispered to him. "I think I am ready to do this on my doggie-own."

"Woof," he whispered back to me. "Yes, you are, my puppy friend. You make me proud."

My puppy raiser soon picked me up into her arms and gently placed me into the kennel for the night.

All the new words I had learned floated around me as I drifted off to sleep.

Side . . . . Under . . . . Up . . . .

Section: Exploring the Community

We went everywhere!

- Stores with yummy smelling food!
- Stores with brightly colored clothes!
- Stores with huge noisy machines!

I walked with pride. My puppy raiser called it socializing. I called it FUN.

On one of our store visits, I waited patiently for her to pay for our items. Suddenly the treat pouch tipped over and kibble spilled onto the floor. People all around watched me, wondering if I might snatch the food up off the floor.

But I showed them! My training had taught me exactly what to do.

I dazzled them with my sit, ignored the food, and kept my eyes on my puppy raiser as she bent over and picked up the food.

She smiled at me proudly. "Good boy, Ely," she said, rewarding me with some kibble

That was so hard, but I am glad my puppy raiser noticed how I remembered my training. I licked my lips between bites. *Mmmm mmmm.*

Section: Traveling Around Town

We took a drive one afternoon to a bus station. Buses are so much bigger and noisier! On all our adventures when I had seen buses pass by, I had wondered, what are they like inside?

My puppy raiser walked me up to the door and encouraged me to take a huge step up to climb the narrow steps inside. We walked through the aisle and she sat down.

"Under," my puppy raiser said. I tucked myself under the seat and faced out.

It was my first bus ride! The engine rumbled underneath my belly, and I bounced up and down.

This is so cool! I wonder where I might go with my partner riding a bus like this?

When the bus stopped, my puppy raiser led me back through the aisle and down the steps. I proudly followed her, feeling I had passed an important test.

After the bus ride, we walked through downtown and my puppy raiser took me to a water fountain. She gave me the command to jump onto its ledge, and then sit.

I could hear gurgling sounds. Water droplets tickled my back.

Umm, I am getting wet. And it is noisy.

But, I stayed for the picture until she told me I was released.

Section: Puppy Class Goes To Duke

Usually our training classes took place at a local store. However, one day my puppy class was invited to a Duke University program where students study how puppies learn.

I got to be part of the testing, and lay on a special mat filled with circles and a box.

The box was for puppies to sit inside, and the circles were for the teachers to put different things for us to choose between.

I had to choose between an empty bowl, or a bowl filled with food. Can you guess which one I picked?

So far I had ridden a bus and an elevator, walked inside stores and been around lots of people. Every day, I walked taller, with more confidence, by my puppy raiser's side.

I felt *even closer* to being a real service dog.

Chapter 6
Ely Joins the Band

As months passed, the weather turned chilly and leaves exploded into colors. My puppy raiser family began taking me to watch a large group of kids together. They were marching! And they were holding instruments! They were so noisy!

My family called it a marching band. I took in all the sights and sounds.

I was in love!

I wagged my tail excitedly at the crashing cymbals and intense, blaring horns. I became a very unique part of this band since my puppy raiser had children who marched and I was the only dog who came to watch all their events.

- Parades!

The sweet smell of dropped cookie crumbs and salty french fries wafted up from the ground right into my nose as I watched the parade. As always, I proudly ignored all the yummy food on the ground, just like my puppy raiser taught me.

♥ Competitions!

The band played in large competitions with bands from around the state. I would wade through crowds of people like a small fish in a big pond.

Once we went to an event where we climbed so many stairs to watch the band, I felt like I was right under the clouds!

Ba-Ba-Boom played the drums! Oom pah-Oom pah sounded the tubas!

Can you see the tiny dots of the band players way down below me?

♥ Concerts!

Sometimes I even listened to the beautiful music of the band while under a chair in a large, dark auditorium. I waited right next to my puppy raiser's feet.
It was very loud!
But, I am so quiet. I bet no one even knows I am here!

I spent so much time with the band—
I even won an award for the Most Relaxed Band Member during one of the band meetings.

Does this mean I can march in the next parade?

During the meeting, my puppy raiser massaged my ears, my belly, and all of my paws. Even with so many people around, a snuggle was top on my list of favorite things to do.

I loved being included in watching the band. Being around their music took me a while to get used to, but after watching and listening to the marching band performing for months, I was not bothered by loud noises or sudden sounds—an important trait for a future service dog.

At then end of those long band-filled days, I snuggled with my family's future band member.

"I hope someday I will see you march in the band too," I whispered to him.

Chapter 7
Ely's Escapades

When I was not practicing commands or working in my vest, I was just part of my puppy raiser's family. I walked to the bus stop on school days, I charged through the leaf piles outside, and I curled up next to the kids when they did homework.

Sometimes we went places where it was bustling with people. I would lay under the bench in the shade, settled and content to be with my puppy raiser. Being with her always made my heart happy.

I also did some other pretty cool stuff!

What cool stuff do you like to do?

Section: Cool Stuff

During the one time we had some winter snow flurries, I ate the only snowball around.

Brrrrrrr, my teeth chattered as icy flakes chipped off.

In the summertime, we hiked on long, winding trails and it was very hot.

One day we even hiked to a waterfall! I shivered as waterfall droplets sprinkled on me from behind.

Oooh, that tickles!

But wow, it felt good.

Section: Trips

We took vacations to enjoy cooler temperatures in the North Carolina mountains. On one trip, I felt the car stop after winding around the mountain roads. I stretched my legs as I hopped out of the car. I trotted over to the grass and sat down.

I am so high up! It reminded me of being at the top of the slide during my puppy playpen days. I fondly remembered those days playing with my brothers and sisters.

I wonder what my brothers and sisters are doing right now?

Click! Sounded the camera. My puppy raiser smiled at me and said, "You are such a handsome boy, Ely!"
She makes me feel like I am her world.

Section: "Learning "Speak"

Many afternoons were spent outside with my puppy raiser while she planted flowers.

I spent my time watching the huge birds nearby. They were called turkey vultures.

Those birds would be so cool to talk with.

"Speak!" My puppy raiser encouraged me. *She can hear my inner most thoughts!* She bounced on her feet and acted really excited.

Speak? I would love to, but how? I really wanted to talk to the birds and make her happy, but did not understand what to do. I just looked at her and wagged my tail happily. Soon she just said "Here," a command that I knew really well. I came right to her and sat down.

"You are such a good boy, Ely!" she said as she fed me kibble.

Puppy Raisers always make sure to end training with their puppy being successful.

Maybe next time I will talk with the birds. I continued crunching on my treats.

My favorite thing of all was snuggling up in the laps of my puppy raiser, and for that matter, anyone who happened to sit on the floor.

I wonder if my future partner will like to cuddle as much as me?

Chapter 8
At Home With My Puppy Raiser

Even though we visited lots of places to practice, being at home was an important part of my training too. Some days we did not go anywhere in the car—we snuggled on the rug together, or I lay next to her as she ate lunch. I even just sat listening as the kids practiced reading their homework out loud.

Section: Working At Home

Occasionally I felt the vest slip gently over me and we 'went to work' in the kitchen. I was told 'bed,' which meant to go under the desk and lay on my mat.

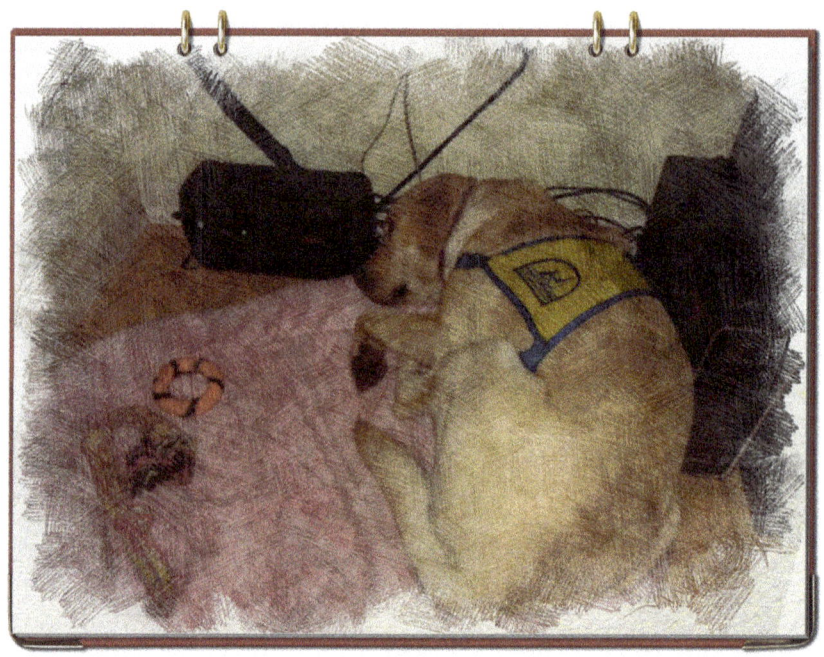

My puppy raiser always made sure I had a few toys with me, but I usually just fell asleep. Sometimes I felt her gently stroking my back. Other times she gave me a command to 'visit.' When she asked me to visit, I promptly nestled my head in her lap.

I love that even when we do not leave the house, I feel I am still needed.

Section: Fun at Home

One warm, spring day, I smelled excitement in the air as my puppy raiser put on my vest. She led me outside with Brisco, and he and I sat together in the driveway, eager to see what she seemed so happy about.

Within minutes—

Cars streamed by. *Beep beep!*

Streamers and balloons floated past me. *Whoosh!*

People cheered. *Woot! Woot!*

It was a car parade celebration for the end of the school year!

"We love your costumes, Brisco and Ely!" Teachers shouted as they drove by.

Wow! Brisco and I are famous!

Section: Volunteering

My puppy raiser and I also had a routine job. Every week, we went to a store where she sorted through hundreds of books. There was nothing for me to help with, being four feet and all.

So, I settled quietly on my mat and watched. Every once in a while, she would slip me a treat for being so well behaved. Sometimes I gnawed on a chew toy or just fell asleep, snoring loudly.

My puppy raiser made sure to remind people I was there when they heard me snoring because they thought SHE was the one making all that noise!

During our time at the store, everyone knew I was working and just smiled at me as they walked by.

Section: Always, Always Learning

My stomach always told me when it was time for dinner by rumbling really loud. I sat still, and patiently waited for my puppy raiser to notice me.

Um, I think it is dinner time? Hello? Like lots of kibble in a bowl?

Crunch crunch? I'm here? Hello?

Really, I could have eaten around the clock. I learned to be patient and wait for my puppy raiser, kindly leaving a puddle of drool as I sat. She just smiled at me and wiped it up with a towel, giving me a kiss when she was done.

One time while she was getting my dinner ready, my puppy raiser held a mound of kibble in her hands and acted extra excited. She knew I was hungry, and spoke that same word from before—the one I didn't understand.

"Ely! Speak!" She even barked at me a few times—*Ruff! Ruff!!*

Hmmm. So I opened and closed my mouth a few times, but no bark came out. She looked disappointed.

What did I not do right?

She dumped the handful of kibble in my bowl and said happily, "You tried, Ely, good boy. Okay!"

I knew that OKAY was the dinner command! *Yummm!*

Some days there was no learning, just plain silliness.

This is embarrassing. I will admit though that it was super soft, so I fell asleep.

There were so many things my puppy raiser and I did together that helped me prepare for my future as a service dog.

Is it time for my next step?

Chapter 9
Next Step-Professional Training

Days passed–547 to be exact. Over 3,000 puppy naps. Each day had been full of walks and field trips…and most importantly…

Snuggling!

What has been your favorite part of Ely's training so far?

Section: Ely Shows He Is Ready

I followed my puppy raiser from room to room. When she was sitting and working on something, sometimes I sat and stared at her, waiting for something to do.

Can I keep you company?

Can I help with that?

How about that?

"Oh Ely," she said to me as she rubbed my ears. "You are ready for your partner, aren't you?"

Yes! I realized. *Wow! I really am!*

I reflected back on all I had experienced.

- Puppy play with my brothers and sisters
- Brisco encouraging me when I was nervous
- Commands my puppy raiser taught me
- Field trips to so many places

I became the confident sidekick I am today because of the amazing community who helped. So many people had whispered to me along the way that I was going to be a great service dog.

My puppy raiser was always telling me she was proud of me—you know what?

I was proud of myself too.

I was excited for my future as a service dog.

Will I still be able to snuggle with someone?

Section: Celebrating before

Before heading away to professional training, we spent quality time together doing our favorite things—outdoor lunches, long walks on mountain trails. It was warm during one hike so I thought I would cool off by dipping my paws in the bubbling creek water. On one hike, I wanted to cool off by putting my paws in the bubbling creek water.

Brrrrrr. I lifted my paws back out of the creek. *This is cold!*
"Ely, sit." I heard. *Whoa! Really?*
But I might turn into a pup-sicle!

I walked back into the water and wiggled my butt carefully and slowly down into the cold, clear water and sat for my puppy raiser.

Even my tail floated!

"Good boy, Ely!" My puppy raiser giggled as she gave me some treats. "That must have been hard for you!" I may have had a cold bottom, but yep, I happily ate my kibble.

It was worth it!

Section: A Special Morning

On our last morning together, my puppy raiser gently slid my vest on. She backed up to take a picture.

I looked away from her, feeling a little confused. I smelled something different within her—I could smell both joy and sadness at the same time.

I knew leaving my puppy raisers would be hard, but I was excited to see what I would learn to help my future forever partner.

The sun had barely risen as everyone hurriedly packed up the car. Every inch of space was filled for our long trip. My food! Blanket! Kennel! All of them went in.

It was exhausting watching them pack!

When the car was filled to the top, everyone took a deep breath–even me!

Before we left, there was an extra-long snuggle session.

I wagged my tail wildly to let them know I was happy with what they had done for me. *My puppy raiser and her family have taught me so much. I think the snuggle time was my favorite.*

It was now time for us to travel to Orlando, Florida for my professional training.

Have you ever travelled on a really long car ride?

Section: Journey to a New Life

The long journey to Orlando began. It was July 19, 2020. We drove in the car for hours—I took over a dozen puppy naps. I sniffed twenty-six dog backyards, seven coffee shops (my puppy raisers' favorite hangout) and many outdoor grills cooking. Their smells wafted into my puppy dreams. When we finally stopped and got out, I saw other people waiting with dogs who looked just like me. The dogs were even wearing the same vest!

Their scents were oddly similar to me.

I wonder if we are all here for the same reason?

I felt my puppy raiser slip a crisp, new vest over my head and clip under my belly. I knew this meant I had reached the next step of my journey to become a service dog.

The soft, blue vest fit perfectly.

My puppy raiser and family took lots of pictures as they gave me hugs and kisses. I peeked over their shoulders and looked across the parking lot.

A huge white van was parked with the doors open. The van had pictures of different dogs wearing the same vest as mine. I knew this ride was meant for me!

I saw several kennels inside, just waiting for a puppy like me to hop in for the ride.

So, I did! This was it!
Can you see me?
I peeked through the door and heard my puppy raiser and family calling out to me.

"We love you Ely!"

"Keep on snuggling, Ely!"

I watched as they got farther and farther away as my new friends and I drove into the distance. My heartstrings tugged a bit. I was sad to see them leave, even though I was excited for what might come next.

I would always remember my time with the band, my trips around the town and most of all, snuggle time with all the family members.

Though I could see tears on their cheeks as they got farther away, I knew they would always remember the confident and handsome boy that had become part of their family.

Next time you see me, my thoughts carrying to them as they got farther away, *I will be a working service dog.*

Chapter 10
Ely's Perfect Match

While my puppy raiser waited at home to hear about my progress, I lived at the school where my professional training took place. There was a room to sleep in, a special eating area, and best of all… special toys and equipment to play on–just like when I was a puppy!

I was among many dogs who were learning new things, just like me. There were several trainers who worked there as well.

How do you feel when you've practiced hard for something and it's finally time?

I even had a roommate, Ion!

Ion was from the "I" litter. We became fast friends, just like Brisco and I had been. We were excited to begin this adventure together.

Section: Professional Training

My trainer, Bryana, was assigned a group of dogs called a 'string.' We took turns working with her. Bryana was the best and she worked with several dogs at a time. First we practiced commands we already knew.

We were pros! Puppy raisers from all over the country had helped every one of us be where we were today.

Remember how hard it was for me and my brothers and sisters to sit still for a picture when we were little?

Sitting still for a picture now was easy-peasy for us older dogs!

Can you guess which incredible dog is me?

We all went on field trips with Bryana at different times to practice our skills and learn new commands, just like we had with our puppy raisers.

Next, she began putting commands together. We heard old ones mixed with some new ones we had just learned. When it was my turn, I heard my name first, followed by a command. Then another. Then another.

I did them all, one after another—even the new command I had just learned!

1. Ely, Stand
2. Ely, Tug
3. Ely, Back

I wrapped my mouth around the rope and pulled really hard to open the door.

Creeeeeeeeeak.

This made me feel so strong! I walked back to the other dogs with a little strut of pride in my step.

What do you think I might use the Tug command for?

Section : Fun Times At Training

I bonded really well with my trainer and knew she was working very hard to prepare me for my forever partner.

My new friends loved Bryana as much as I did, and learned along with me during our training. They were looking for forever partners too!

We put our noses in Bryana's lap and gave her puppy love eyes during our break times.

We ALL loved practicing the 'visit' command with her and feeling gentle head rubs, and hearing her soft words of encouragement.

We celebrated our success with puppy play and snuggle time several times a day.

You do remember how much I loved my snuggle time, right?

At school, Bryana and the other trainers had fun times with us too. Our training took place over several months, so I was there for Halloween and Thanksgiving–even my second birthday!

Bryana took special care to dress me during the holidays, too.

I looked so dashing in the antlers and festive greenery she put me in for the seasonal pictures.

I wonder if flying lessons are included in my training too?

Section: Ely Finally Speaks

During training one morning, I heard that familiar word 'speak' again. Bryana was saying it to my roommate, Ion, and you know what he did? He barked!

Is that what my puppy raiser was trying to get me to do? I did not know I could bark for helping as a service dog!

I jumped up and down a little. I was so excited and my front legs hopped, tail wagging, trying to get Bryana's attention.

She looked over at me.

"Ely," she said. "Speak!" And I barked! Her eyes lit up and she smiled.

I even barked three times in a row when she asked me to 'speak' again! I was so happy!

She gave me a big hug and said how proud she was of how hard I had worked for that one command.

Section: Team Training

Months passed and then it was time for team training, where we would all meet our future partner. Many people had been waiting months for a service dog and travelled a long way to the school hoping to find their perfect match. Bryanna partnered me with several different people to watch how we worked together.

Sometimes I was led by a tall man through the halls as he practiced commands with me. Other times I walked calmly next to a woman who was wearing a leg brace.

When she sat on the floor one day to take a rest, I lay on her legs to rest too.

I heard her telling me about all the adventures we would go on if I was her partner. Zoos and aquariums and so much more!

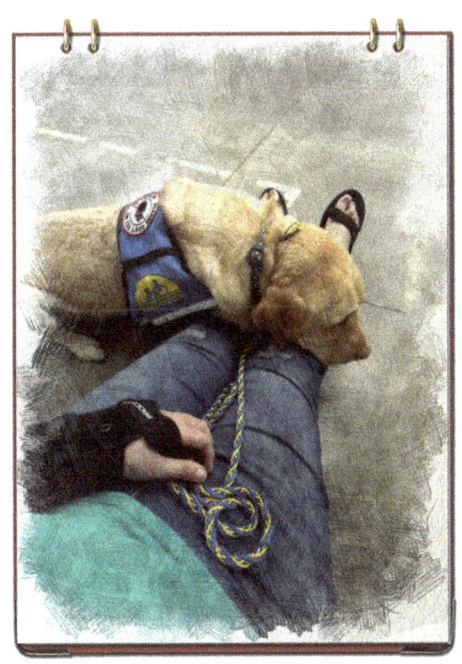

She told me I was handsome and such a good boy.

I wagged my tail happily as I listened to her. I felt like I could stay with her forever.

Section: My Forever Partner

The air was charged with extra excitement one day. I could feel it in the air. Today was the day! February 12, 2021. I was going to be officially matched with my forever person.

Who would it be?

I walked into our training room and saw my person across the room. It was the young lady with the leg braces. My partner's name was Miranda. I knew she was the one meant for me because every time I looked at her, her eyes were filled with love, and hope.

Miranda called me handsome.

She whispered she loved me.

The best thing about my new partner? She loved having me lay across her legs with my head in her lap and well… you KNOW I am a snuggler.

We were made for each other.

We spent an entire week practicing together and getting to know each other. I showed her how much I could help her.

I picked up her room key because it was hard to bend over from the wheelchair.

I stood solid next to her when she pulled herself up to walk.

I *always* held the door open for her.

Every night, she invited me up on the bed with her and we snuggled while she watched TV. This is what I had dreamed about from the very beginning.

I was her service dog, and we graduated as a team on February 18, 2021.

Section: Reunited

Before we went to my new home, Miranda brought me into a special room where I heard voices. These weren't just any voices. I heard voices from my puppy life!

Wait…is it?? Really?

It was my puppy raiser family! They were not in the room with me, but I could hear them through the computer, talking to Miranda. Their voices were filled with excitement when they saw me.

Then I heard, "Woof." I heard it again, louder this time, "Woof!"

Brisco! He was with my puppy raiser family to congratulate me too!

Wow. Everyone I love is here with me to celebrate.

I felt so content, like my world was complete.

All their love and help along the way helped me be the best I could be. Everyone was so proud of me! Most of all, I knew I had accomplished something amazing. My heart soared and my tail swished back and forth with joy.

Before I knew it, my trainer was saying goodbye to me. Miranda loaded me into her car. I knew I was right where I was supposed to be, snuggled in safely with my partner—the one with the love-eyes.

Miranda looked at me with a smile and said, "Let the adventures begin!"

Note From the Author

Ely was with our family for nineteen months—January 2019 until July 2020. During the last five months of his training with us, the pandemic was a full on mess, but I chose not to emphasize that during this story. There were months when puppy classes were virtual and we practiced commands in an empty, once vibrant downtown. Ely adapted very well to the change in routines and I chose to weave images taken during that time into his overall journey of being a service dog puppy.

We met Ely's partner Miranda virtually when she graduated in February of 2021, but it was almost a year before we finally met in person.

Meeting Miranda in December of 2021 was truly a blessing. She is an amazing young lady and we were able to also see (and of course share a quick snuggle with) Ely again.

Miranda and Ely are truly meant to be together.

Thank you for adding Ely, Life As A Service Dog Puppy to your library. If you and your child enjoyed this story, please consider posting a thoughtful review on Amazon, Goodreads or other favorite book site. Your kindness will make a difference for others considering this book.

Proceeds from *Ely, Life As A Service Dog Puppy* are donated to Canine Companions® to assist in providing training for present and future service dogs.

Did I catch your attention?

Canine Companions® dogs can be trained to perform a variety of tasks. Let me tell you about the different types of assistance dogs they train!

- Service Dogs
- Hearing Dogs
- Skilled Companions
- Facility Dogs
- Service Dogs for Veterans
- Therapy Dogs

Canine Companions service dogs and all follow-up services are free.

Amazing, right?

Puppy Talk!

Puppy, Puppy, Puppy: Birth through 8 weeks

What is a Breeder Caretaker? *Breeder Caretakers are volunteers who provide specially bred mom and dad dogs a healthy and happy home. When caring for a female who has a litter of puppies, these volunteers raise and socialize puppies per Canine Companions® early care protocols.*

What is a "litter?" *A litter refers to the number of puppies born at the same time by the same female dog. All the brothers and sisters make up a 'litter.' All Canine Companions puppies born in the same litter have a name that begins with the same letter!*

Birth order and collar color—*Each puppy is given a different colored ribbon when they are born. Ribbon colors represent the order in which puppies are born, and help keep track of the puppies as they grow. They all look so much alike!*

Puppy Raiser Time

What is a Puppy Raiser? *Puppy raisers are volunteers that take a puppy into their home and provide love, care, training and socialization until it is time for professional training.*

Why is it so important for a puppy to 'speak'? *Barking can be a valuable tool to get help. If someone with a disability is home alone and happens to fall down or need other assistance, they could give their service dog the command to 'speak' to get the attention of someone nearby.*

How long is a puppy with a raiser? *A puppy stays with their puppy raiser anywhere from fourteen to twenty months.*

Training Tools

What is the purpose of the training vest? *When puppies wear their vest, it tells those around them that they are working. The vest has special words on it that say 'future service dog.'*

Why is the kennel used? *If a puppy is not able to be supervised, they relax in the kennel so they cannot get into mischief! The kennel becomes a puppy's special retreat, and they find comfort being in it.*

Harness/Gentle Leader®—*A Gentle Leader® is a training tool that gently guides the dog without pulling on its neck. Ely is wearing a blue gentle leader in several of the pictures.*

And finally: Ely

Do all CC dogs like to snuggle as much as Ely? *Not all dogs are snugglers, just like not all people like to hug! Ely was not unique in loving to cuddle but it helped him be a perfect fit for Miranda.*

What can a business ask?

"Is the dog a service animal required because of a disability?"

"What work or task has the dog been trained to perform?"

Learn more at: cci.org/stopfraud

A SERVICE DOG IS MORE THAN A VEST™

Type of Dog	Definition	Access Rights	Training Required	What to Do If the Animal Is Misbehaving
Assistance/ Service Dog	A dog trained in specific tasks that mitigate the handler's disability.	Permitted with handler in any place the public is allowed.	Extensively trained to perform specific tasks to mitigate effects of handler's disability.	Must be in control at all times and behave in a safe manner. Aggression or continued misconduct can result in the dog's removal under the ADA.
Puppy in Training	A dog that is learning tasks for a handler with a disability or for a program that provides service dogs.	With permission. Rely on goodwill of businesses for access to prepare the puppy for service. Some state laws permit equal access.	In the process of training and socialization to mitigate the effects of disability.	Must be in control at all times and behave in a safe manner. Puppies in training rely on the goodwill of businesses for access, but can be removed.
Emotional Support Animal	A dog or other animal whose sole function is to provide comfort or provide emotional support to its owner with a disability.	Only allowed in owner's home, college dormitories and airplanes as outlined in Fair Housing Act and Air Carrier Access Act.	Basic manners expected but none required by law.	Can be removed.
Therapy Animal	A temperament-tested pet providing comfort in an approved facility.	Only with permission at designated facility.	Basic obedience and sound temperament expected but not required.	Can be removed.

Acknowledgements

Ely is one of thousands of graduated service dogs since the founding of **Canine Companions**®.

Canine Companions is leading the service dog industry so that their clients and their dogs can live with greater independence. They provide service dogs to adults, children and veterans with disabilities and facility dogs to professionals working in healthcare, criminal justice and educational settings.

Since their founding in 1975, their dogs and all follow-up services are provided at no cost to their clients.

Independence shouldn't be limited to those who look or live a certain way. Disability reaches all races, classes and backgrounds, and Canine Companions will too. Clients come to Canine Companions because of their reputation, the quality of their dogs, the experience of their training staff and the desire to lead life with greater independence. They are committed to providing services to all qualified clients.

For additional information on Canine Companions, please visit: https://canine.org/

In Chapter 5, Ely went on a field trip with his puppy friends to visit the Duke Canine Cognition Center and its Puppy Kindergarten program.

The Duke Puppy Kindergarten program is a longitudinal study funded by the National Institute of Health to assess the impact of different rearing strategies on the behavior and cognitive development of assistance dogs. The goal of the program is to increase the supply of assistance dogs and to see more dogs graduate and serve more people.

Each semester, over a hundred Duke undergraduates help raise puppies from Canine Companions® from 8-20 weeks of age. The students also run the puppies through a range of cognitive games that will function as a kind of early aptitude testing, which will be used in the future as early identifiers of puppies who are most likely to graduate as assistance dogs.

To learn more about the Duke program, please visit:

https://evolutionaryanthropology.duke.edu/duke-puppy-kindergarten

Meet the Author

The author with current pup-in-training, Barley, 2022

Margot has trained with over 10 dogs during the last 25 years. She has served as a puppy raiser for nine service dogs as well as worked with therapy dogs. She firmly believes that all dogs have a purpose and that belief has propelled her to volunteer in multiple dog placement programs that service communities.

Ely, Life As A Service Dog Puppy is her second children's story in the series Tails of Dogs Who Help. The first book in the series, *Brisco, Life As A Therapy Dog*, tells the story of Brisco's work in the community helping others. In telling the stories of the many dogs she has raised, she is excited to teach the message of what our dogs can do for us– whether it be through therapy or through service. The author's hope is these books will be a fun way to educate kids about how these dogs become who they are meant to be by telling it through the eyes of the dog.

Margot Bennett is based in North Carolina and married with four children. When she's not working with dogs, helping with homework, or volunteering at schools, you can find her hiking, swimming, or hiding out in her nook working on scrapbooking, playing the drums and dreaming of when her next service dog puppy will arrive.

She is excited to be working on her third book in the series.

Rocky, Life As A Guide Dog will be available soon.

Want to learn more?

Visit Margot's website
dogswhohelp.com

Follow all the Bennett dogs on Instagram!
@tailsofdogswhohelp
#tailsofdogswhohelp

and on Facebook:
facebook.com/Tails-Of-Dogs-Who-Help

Coming Soon!

The next book in the series

Tails Of Dogs Who Help
Book 3

Rocky, Life As A Guide Dog

Meet Rocky, a handsome yellow Lab who tells the story of his journey becoming a guide dog. Follow his life from puppy born of the R litter, to training with Margot as his puppy raiser, and finally into advanced training at Guiding Eyes For the Blind, where he finds the perfect match to work with as a guide dog.

www.ingramcontent.com/pod-product-compliance
Lightning Source LLC
Chambersburg PA
CBHW061147170426
43209CB00011B/1589